MOVING TO WALES

AND OTHER POEMS

NOEL WOODIN

MOVING TO WALES

AND OTHER POEMS

PRESELI EDITIONS 1996

First Published in 1996 by
Ancient Landscapes
Teg y Pistyll
Glanrhyd
Dyfed SA43 3PA

© Noel Woodin

All rights reserved etc.

Set, Printed and Bound by
CIT Printing Services
Haverfordwest,
Dyfed.

ISBN 0 9523570 0 3

PRINTED IN WALES

Some of these poems have appeared previously in the following magazines and the author would like to thank their editors. Botteghe Oscura, (Rome). The London Magazine. New Statesman. Time and Tide. Nimbus. And some have been broadcast on the BBC Third Programme, and on various regional programmes. Again thanks. The cover is from a painting by Tony Steele-Morgan of a cottage of the Welsh harpist. Daffydd A`r Garreg Wen. The author wishes to thank Tony Steele-Morgan for permission to reproduce the painting.

CONTENTS *Page Numbers*

Moving to Wales	9
A Man One Morning	18
Learning Dry-stone Walling	21
The Angler Rests	23
Riverman	24
Origin of Rivers	25
Being Upon Hills	26
Variations For The Newly Loved	27
Rhapsody In Blue	30
The Beech Tree	31
Mushrooms	32
Poem For His Children When Young	33
Affirmation	36
A Stranger Late Frost	38
Two Sonnets	39
Such An Evening That The Sky	41
Three Landscapes For The Solitary	42

MOVING TO WALES

1

They told me it would be cold and they were right.
I awoke that first morning and could see
The icefern scrolled on the window-light.
I spoke in a cumulus proceeding me.
But arctic monologues were wasted, cast
On hard-gained solitude, that sine qua non.
I lit the kitchen fire. Ready at last
For silence, that shelf you put words on.

I saw I'd change just be being there.
In day-long silences you find yourself
Unhindered, re-forming, unaware
Of process and design. That very shelf
Has all the aspects of a well-appointed home,
Has a kind of quiet intention to become.

2

Builders style it 'rustic'. The walls are stone,
Random-coursed, rough-pointed and so thick
Windows are set in tunnels. Little's shown
Of the mason's cultured art except the trick
(Or greater art) of using this and that
Just where and as it is. So it seems grown
As if by husbandry more than built,
Is rooted deeply in, not squatting on.

Outside, an elm. It is dead, white as bone,
Strangely whiter now at night when lit
By light shed from that bright, well-trodden moon
And foxy shadows flicker into it.
Or are they real? I do not feel alone
But sense those Chinese eyes, slitted to glint.

3

There's water in the tap - comes from a spring
'Gravity fed'. It falls, I guess is meant.
It's soft as flour though soap suds tend to cling.
Otherwise, benign this element.
For fire there's wood. When split, green ash is white
As thighs. And it burns well. Slowest is oak
But thorn is best for heat. To mix is right.
We are Red Indians, know by smoke
For I've distant neighbours whose chimneys write
Thin calligraphy on local skies.
And I write back. I have not met them yet.
There might be things to say. Behind my eyes
I rehearse some greetings. I will try
My fledgling Welsh, a cheeping, shy 'sut mae`?*

(*: Pronounced in Pembrokeshire 'shoo my` means, how is it going?)

4

In learning languages, the little word
Tends to perplex. How prepositions loom
Big as buses but blank. I have been heard
To say 'on' a tafarn, 'under' a room
And all of it is put so haltingly.
Tongue-tied, unfluent, though the head is full,
Lacking those charming childhood graces we
Are geriatrics in a nursery school.

We know too much to learn. with the ease
Of the osmotic absorbing innocent.
But three words for 'yes' and like complexities
Get mastered: at last you say what's meant
Until a rush of words shows how you lack
A basic skill - what has been said back?

5

I'm trying to learn and sometimes understand,
(Nothing to be hurried though sloth's the crime)
The pull and the demand that is the land.

All is urgent, nothing is freely gained -
Even common grass needs a feed of lime.
I'm trying to learn and sometimes understand

That you must also watch, forget the grand
Idea, or merely say, 'When there is time'.
The pull and the demand that is the land -

There's arrogance in thinking you command,
That you're in control like making rhyme.
I'm trying to learn and sometimes understand

How much must simply happen. Forcing and
Man-marking fail. Defeat's trail of slime.
The pull and the demand that is the land

Means earthquakes' always near at hand,
Mole miniature, a maddening pantomime.
I'm trying to learn and sometimes understand
The pull and the demand that is the land.

6

I read the birdbook more than books by Dunn
And Graham (a brace of Scots for company),
For the sky`s a freehold fought in, flown
By a property-owning anarchy.
I try to identity before they`re gone
Those startling finches, flickering into fire
And one that cowers, pretending to be stone
Below the risen buzzard, blasé in air.

Why do this? The essential fact of wren
Gains nothing from nomenclature, still is
Itself, whether named or anonymous,
A mere tea-spoon of a bird. Naming then,
Is greed, claim-staking efforts to possess.
It`s theft by enclosure: or by pen.

7

The early jay has a rachet in its throat
That would awaken a two-bottle man.
And so one morning I too went out
Into the blear, birdclocked to a plan.

For birds provoke ideas. I have two bogs
Where tussock reed's the only thing to see.
A heron flew off, sated perhaps with frogs
And I came alive with a great discovery -

My wealth is liquid. You see, it`s all about
Marsh equals water and water equals lake:
Thence, that one-time adversary - trout.
So I`m all History small. Domesticate
The prey and city culture starts. No doubt
The nomads suffered. Surely, this one won`t.

8

Sometimes Welsh rain begins by standing still
In grey cobwebs of sky, hanging down.
You barely feel it broaden out until
It has. And is relentless as monsoon.

I should be digging but petered up by rain
I serve some kitchen-time old laggedly
And stare out, an inhabitant within
Obliquer impulses, contrary.

Why are moods so rarely congruent?
I feel bardic when the weather's good
But turn farmer when the black south-west
Walks in. Well, we all know how it would
Be facile otherwise. Forcing is an Art
Releasing mood, it lets the old lag out.

9

Cwm Cerwyn, Cwnc Rhudd and Foel Feddau *
Were once to me no more than names on maps.
Now, where I live. Maybe, where I'll die
Though that`s no solemn thought. More so, perhaps -
And I sense the beginnings of complacency -
Has been a strange realisation that
Unaware of process, it`s plain to see
I`ve found myself with everything I want.

I`m hardly used to it yet. Of course, it`s not
Pride of possession - that merely builds a tomb,
But more my own words coming true. It`s what
I said. The shelved, well-appointed home
Has produced a new inhabitant.
That quiet intention has in deed become.

*Pronounced: Coombe Ker-win, Koonock Reeth, Voyel Veth-eye.

A MAN ONE MORNING

The village bark against intruder light
And my cover, night, was gone. Alone,
Yes, I'll act. There are things to do
As morning sees herself in mirrors that
Leave a white reflection on the dew.

So I squander sight - the spread of land.
Of falcon levels, the distant, smoking town,
This morning early. As I move my hand
Flowers are other people on their own
Who move away. I would not be sad.

And seemingly my attitude is right,
The challenge of the manifested light.

2

In the vast dormitory of ideas
A gipsy partnered speech. He went his way
As the early lark showed him how high
The sky could really be. He learned to say
That soft idiom of feathers. His avid eye
Travelled through hedges where it tamed a wren
And found the spider circuses spread out
In bracken places. And it was morning then.
A huge complexity had come about.

In the forges, the foundries of this light
A worker spoke. His boasting tongue gave birth.
His eye was every place that light became,
Though weasel stratagems were done by stealth
In hidden tracks, where whispers could be rain,
His eye held places still. His presence spoke
As one with natural doctrine, in the same
Revolutions named. As that morning broke
A thunderous sunlight came and armies woke.

In arsenals of petal, breath and fur
An espionage of language told the spy
How poems live on lips, how heroes are
Governed by their responsibility.
How it is a striding forth, yet done
Within the tiny room of poetry
To make a place that even now is moving on.
And the dream? - it is to say that things will be
Just what they are but with authority.

3

This is my own act. No one asks me why,
Nor cares. My words are a lonely spoken act.
My tears are a passing gesture. And if I sigh
My neighbour bears me not. Even if I want.

It is to be the abstract quality
Of music. There is no future but
A bird`s. And more I do not need to see.
Indeed, I cannot see more than that.

Anyway why? I would rather leave
A soft proposition of insight on your tongue
In which the idiomatic starlings weave
A way of fixing light. I would not wrong
The essential fact of wrens. I say no more
And wonder who is this man who says he saw.

Each man has mystery. This is the law.

LEARNING DRY-STONE WALLING

in memoriam 'Burglar` Denley, Esq

His nickname came about through a lady in the village who had managed to lock herself out of her new bungalow. 'Burglar` was passing and being a true countryman had many useful objects about his person. Selecting a piece of wire he quickly picked the lock and stood back expecting praise for his efforts. But she said, "You`re nothing more than a burglar. I`m going to call the police``. He fled. But the name stuck.

Remember when the five-pound note
Was white, a page of scripted copperplate?
(You had to sign the back). He would boast
Of autographing sessions that
Made profligacy into an Art

And demanding drink a right
I could not dispute. And this I paid.
For in that distant rural vie boheme
There was a sense of rank. My grade
Was new boy yet to make my name.

Anyway, money should never spoil a drink.
I`d learned that in the Soho school
Circa early Fifties. And thus I think
I was tested and found suitable.
For anyone really can do the work

But can you endure the worker? Say
A wall`s so long, yes, say about a chain
To be capped perhaps in 'cock and hen`
From footings till you draw your pay
Can take the best part of a week.

So you`ve to know how silence is
When you must nod, when you should speak.
You fall into a trance but still respect
Each others` stream of consciousness
That may surface oddly. There`s etiquette

Where the work is almost periphereal.
And this? Well, you make an outer shell
Of larger stone, coursed and even faced
As is warranted by price. The fill
Is rubble, not tipped but gently placed

For a wall is like a fragile cage
Until it`s finished. It`s much like Art
In this, well worth stressing when the wage
Is mooted. And luck can play a part.
You`ll strike a stone a casual hammer blow

And lo! it breaks into a quoin you hoard,
Because a corner is a crucial stage,
A datum point you work toward
Or from. In the courses you look below
To span the joint and wedge it tight

Just by habit: but cornerstones are thought.
Soft stone is best (insides like herring roe)
As hard stone shatters and will tegulate.
But this is relative. Both can hurt
Like buggary if dropped upon your feet.

So it`s really putting stone on stone until
It`s high and long enough: simply that.
You learn it quick or you never will -
There`s instinct in the simplest artefact -
And it`s good to know you`ve got it still,

Unossified by Education and
Mere market forces. Bravura begs
No favours, you`re the swaggering artisan,
The steeple-jack with his jangling frogs,
The lampheaded miner, the found working man.

So, dressed in my scruff, donkey-jacket and hat,
The cleggéd boot that sometimes sparked a stone,
I coalesced and classed, was not an act,
Joining a human construct. Not alone
Had become again my new inhabitant.

THE ANGLER RESTS

Under a lens of sky
I'm a tree to that trout
Working a territory. above as well below
The white oils of the pool.
I am breathing out
Gently and am very quiet.
It rides the liquid roads.
I'm in my traffic'd air.

Below there are green strands,
And blue mats, like drowned hair
Cling to rocks. Above, a threat:
But I will let
Hunters be. This is
An encounter of separates
Who, though present, never meet.

RIVERMAN

A river is itself continually:
An Amazon in ditches, estuarine
In hillside waterhatch: dark pools
And green shelves are sea levels
Held and going on. All in one
For the travelled satanic eel,
All in one in the blue minnow world.

This medium in transit speaks to me
For I would flow, mingling a wayward kind
In a merging current: raid dot, foam lace
And waving water hair are the
Welcome forward. And all in one
In the still heron mirror,
All in one in the washed pebble reach.

And so it is in the trickle spring I hear
The tides in deltas. And I would leave
The hearth, the brick, the timber tie
And led by long currents, discover mine.
As if to spend the money in my veins
In one sunlit debauch, and drawing free
Become all one, as rivers are, continually.

ORIGIN OF RIVERS

Is a country maker straightaway
Smoothing rock even where it wells
Breaking the bubble of its waterskins.
You could hold it all
In a cup of hands
And feel a cold forging.

It forms silt dunes and a nest of whorls
Soft as wholemeal as the settled flow
Is a found speed, a true identity.
No bigger than a plate
A scooped pool collects
An inch-high waterfall.

And it`s lived in. Ranunculus has white
Thimbles floating as air and sunlight fix
A liquid chemistry. Minnows scatter
Over the pebbled reach.
Leaving the vestigial egg
Fingerlings find they are fish.

Each bend entices now
And if you follow on
You are some land flotsam
Buckled to the current. Suddenly there
Is a heron pretending a tree. A quick
Grey thrust. The surface yields up. Water resumes

To being what it is,
A maker. It`s always new,
Sparkles to say the white
Sound of sent water falling. And spray
Held in faced air is fine. You breathe within
This drench of molecules whose smell is moss

As it grows into
A stately mover, a queen
In progress and bends
Back a valley, lays out a chequered plain.
Now, it is a country and a money maker,
Delta`d is lost among a raft of towns.

BEING UPON HILLS

I came to cliff-edge and saw
A buzzard stilled in his spiralling,
Profiled to my level eye,
Thin as a juggler`s plate
At the posed apex of air.

Briefly held high, I met
That bird on equal terms
Eye to eye. We shared a breath
Of risen heather scent,
The collisions of a moment

Gone away before it`s found.
For then, that tilt of wings,
The span that stroked a sky
Turned all the horizon round.
We were two dots and distancing.

VARIATIONS FOR THE NEWLY LOVED

So fond. This dawn as raucous birds
Proclaim the freehold they have flown
We are each other`s quiet unknown
To make toward: wherein these words.

And with them, we unfolding, learn
The silent idiom of lust
With open looks: a naked trust
Forms the strength of a shared concern.

A rare conjunction! I see it break
Me from me till I`m no more
He who spoke my words before.
And find myself as stranger, wake

And breathe an awkward origin
So new. A future is at hand,
Charted with just each other and
Our vast achievement to begin.

2

Come then, my gentle stranger, where these flowers
Are signposts to a way: wherein I see
Something of a sweet nobility
Now the common motive`s found. It powers

A carefree project. Think of nothing more
But that an instant leads to, perhaps
Much further than we thought. There are no maps
That have us shown, although we saw

Through the private door our fond degree.
Consider what we were and what we are.
Two commitments meet. They shall go far.
How new the old familiar seems to be

And is. Last night the moon disclosed those white
Continents. By whose light you let
Me trace lip journeys till we freshly met
Entwined within the complex writhing knot

That bodies make. Then laughed the night away
On pillow profundities. We were as one,
The vast achievment you and I`ve begun
Is a firm commandment to obey.

3

I see the trembling lawns of barley and
The campion stationed road. It is our way.
It was never told us, never planned.

As now our vast achievement is at hand.
It tells a shared concern that is today.
I see the trembling lawns of barley and

Our way of being writ. We understand
How implications are and we could pay.
It was never told us, never planned.

Nor this strangely changing sky, Now bland,
Now starling livid, now mottled, once grey,
I see the trembling lawns of barley and

A threat, a test to come. But when the band
Of mere enchantment breaks, we`ll still obey.
It was never told us, never planned

The true responsibility, to stand
And be, let common values fall away.
I see the trembling lawns of barley and
It was never told us, never planned.

RHAPSODY IN BLUE

To present and not describe presents
The night. Now over the plum glow
It wanders into earthy apple scents.
I hear an orchard cadence and I go
Where the wind is gentle with nervous trees.
I am some sombre figure and alone.
The old man of night sighingly breathes
Upon this blue September and lies down.

And then, that man of night turns again
Like a river that loses its memory
In the back of your eye. I move on
Involved as a paraded secrecy
That also has the colour of the sloe.
It is a dark invention where badgers blink
And sense their ways. It is a damson blue.
It is the risen silence of the oak.

The lampshadow life in the domestic room
I pass, has a human, nuclear look.
It will not see my eyes. I'm from the dark
Looking in and you cannot call that home.
A footprinted grass bruise, and then I go
Under the risen silence of the oak
In a mole-mauve dingle, where, although
Privacies enclose, you hear them speak.

THE BEECH TREE
in memoriam Sally Curtis-Hayward

It was appropriate then, that bare December day,
A friend, we three and the monolithic beech,
The surely risen wind with the swerving rook away
On a black going. And a solitary grief for each
When the ashes were cast. The brief burial in air,
That fell to the biblical ground. I turned my face
Away to drop a private tear. I did not dare
To speak. The beech became her quiestest place.

But when I went there the other day that tree
Was a green bell. As if to listen I sat below
Uncalm upon he floor. What reminded me?
Was it that which she cannot see? I do not know
The origin of the later tear. Perhaps I search
Among her loss. Or is it my own I trace?
I am like a bee trapped in an empty church
Worn down to wearied silence at the quietest place.

MUSHROOMS
in memoriam Sally Curtis-Hayward

Under the spider canopies spread out
On rich blue grass I saw the first white domes.
I was time-warped, recalled the childrens` shout,
'Mushloom, mushloom, Mummy I see mushlooms!`
Locked in time was, I too shouted it
And an earshot farmer scurried away to give
Me the widest berth. I'll tell you this, I thought,
Forgetting you were dead, remembering how you live.

A POEM FOR HIS CHILDREN WHEN YOUNG

Now here`s a poem for Isabelle,
Here`s one for Peter too.
I wrote it after Sunday lunch
Kippers, rhubarb and stew.

I`d been that morning to see the lakes
That are at Tally Ho.
Isabelle was born there
More than four years ago.

And Peter used to come with me
When 'woodin` we would go.
There was a place too, near a wall,
Where mushrooms used to grow.

I saw the lane where down the hill
Mummy rode her bike:
But Mummy has a mind of her own,
That time, the wall she struck.

She hasn`t really changed a lot.
She`s learning to drive you say.
Watch out! Watch out! You other cars!
`Attends! Vous allez tomber!

Now do you remember Pimbury Park,
The ice, the frost, the snow?
I went quite near the other day
When driving we did go.

The snow it made a raucous rook
A far far blacker bird.
And late at night the hungry fox
Barking could be heard.

I wonder if Peter remembers this.
Isabelle was too small,
Although she`s now a nice-sized girl,
Not tiny nor too tall.

And she will be the dancing girl
At parties she will play
She`ll wear a dress of long blue silk
And shoes of silver grey.

And like the princess in the tale
The princes all will queue
To say to her, 'Me dear, may I
Dance this dance with you`?

And Peter`s six! Now that`s a lot.
One more than five its true,
Two more than four, three more than three,
And four more than two.

And he will be the bravest boy
And wear the coat of love,
Be strong as iron, sweet as milk,
And gentle as the dove.

For he can count far more than ten,
The 'Duke of York` can sing
(Who marched his men to the top of the hill
And he marched them down again).

And I think he knows a funny song
Called Michael Finnegan.
They say he caught a silver fish
And threw it in again.

Well, it`s good to sing a funny song
And to tell a story well,
To write a letter to your dad
With all the news to tell.

You must let me know what you have done
This time I`ve been away,
And when we next, all three meet,
We`ll have so much to say.

For love`s my trade to serve again,
As soon it will be yours.
I hope your way is easier.
Remember - there are no laws.

But when the swan of evening glides
And you are almost asleep,
While high above a steady star
The sky is place does keep.

I think of you both as I hope
You both will think of me
Until we all without a sound
Forget our poetry.

And sleep, my children, sleep to wake
On worlds where we can be,
The laughing, running, happy ones -
Bound, but at liberty.

AFFIRMATION

I have seen the world as it really is
With one idea I went and saw my life in glass
A forest turned a page and I heard the night
Read softly in my ear
A vilage barked in moonlight but
My road was clear.

I have held a violent river in my eyes
Cast it aside
And been tyrannical to owls
Cursed sages with a coin and gave no praise
And after thoughts, my pride
Spurned with anger and went its ways
So anger died

I have hidden wealth in pockets of the clock
And all I gain
I give to flowers, I do not work
A profligate in brothels of the rose
I'm known to entertain
A lady dressed in a lilac`s clothes
And pearls of rain.

I have made maps of unknown places and
Seen lust dictate
Lazy regions to command
A stranger came to know me. A stranger came
And now I celebrate
In other worlds that have my name
The futures wait.

I have heard the winds` glass tongue on nights of frost
Speaks of snow
And diamonds in the sky were lost
In burglaries of cloud. I saw the rook
And silver on the bough
And what I had to say I spoke
I turned to go.

And went where children played and fishes laughed
In harbour foam
Where swallows fell and linnets raved
And through the sky came sounds of blue applause
And blossoms on the plum
And pear obeyed the natural laws
And I came home.

And home was where I started. I have seen
Reality
Where rivers argue, where the green
And waving acres turn to violet land
And I let silence be
A village sleep in midnight and
The rest of me.

A STRANGE LATE FROST

And shall the ice, the fallen iron sky
Disclose a way for seasons to begin?
A brash and thrusting violet shivers in
The absent charities. The north`east wind,
A cold hand, lies on a cringing thigh.

The cheating April has opened doors,
A landlady with an angled, glassy smile
That says a firm denial. This white pause
Snarls at the green rhythms, those laws
That seem to lie. My breath is white a while.

And tonight will be a white event.
What recurrent abstract has defined
The buds that shiver in a green attempt?
And do we ourselves do what we are meant?
My eyes are open yet instinct is blind.

And so I slowly tap my way unplanned
Through formulations of oblique intent,
As if to do what I am meant.

Primroses in the ice cathedrals and
A birdless, sullen sheet that is the sky;
I clearly do not begin to understand
The eccentric green beginnings, nor why.

QUIET TIME AT WATERHATCH

There is a place where plover nestle down
In handshaped hollows and sunlight hardly lies
More than a rim above. There is a huge alone.
Rooks are quiet blots. Nothing flies
Across the standing blue ruin of air.
Sweet like marzipan the maythorn scent
Could almost be eaten. Everywhere
Is secretive and does what is meant.

On these nights when I am walking home
And see the nervous hare all set to run
Yet waiting with tall ears primed, I'm one
Who would not disturb a mouse nor harm
The green underworld. I would not bring
My element to bear on anything.

WILD TIME AT LONGDON

I came by way of Pendock and the Long Green Cross
And the cider fires were blazing down by sight.
Drunken as a blackberry as I was
I heard a foxbark knife the deeps of night.

Who saw me saw one amazed with skies
As dewy globes held on a spier`s line
Stood on my path. I broke them with my eyes.
My feet struck rock and tumbled in the lane.

Who saw me saw no one that I knew
Saw only a boasting hero of a thirst
And several graver things I did'nt do.
Though I was garrulous, was one of the best,
Who spurned the suburban cosies, laughed all through
Their tidy roads, I went as one much blessed

SUCH AN EVENING THAT THE SKY

Such an evening that the sky
Was a woman`s ample bosom;
And under it I
(Given to the trades of definition)
Walked through the fine dusk blossom.

A dealer in infinities;
Elated like a great seducer
I had the ease
Of clouds that pass the starry pack.
The campion held the winter back.

And evening hummed by the sleeping bee
Became my throne
No dispute spoke for I could be
The paramount concern: alone
A man becomes his complexity.

And the splendid chapel of the night
Emptied of worshippers, dissolved
Its starry dome.
I was dethroned, in sleep resolved,
And, like the prodical, came home.

THREE LANDSCAPES FOR THE SOLITARY

``a good picture must seem to go beyond its frame`` Robert Coloquhuon

1

And on the further side, almost leaning
A perched farm works its awkward land.
Sheep move. Then they are there. They are
Always in the right place when you look.

A hawk lands on the wires and becomes
A cruel army emblem held up high.
There will be uproar soon. Even now,
Placid seeming, it is never still.

And the quiet place scattered with broken shells
Has the hint of something quite sudden
About to happen. It will not while you are
Within. You will not see enactment here.

Thus the unfound worm, the formed head
Held fast to fern, are intermediate
And, as I am, defined by other eyes,
Placid seeming, incorporate, not still.

2

The brimstone butterfly
Sulphurs a slender blade.
I yawn. My crush of grass
The only mark I've made.

A day to pleasure the skin
In feather airs. And lie,
Let breezes trail my arm
Like a waterfly.

And be no one. Merely
A prone, habit machine
That idles, below thinking,
An uneasy go-between.

The brimstone butterfly
Sulphurs a slender blade.
I am uninvolved.
This is a choice I made.

3

Imagine living here in winter say.

You hear the quiet of snow before it`s seen,
Before the curtain`s drawn a prescience tells
How it is blinding white. And it is still.
It is so still. The drifts are structured wind.
They are made air. Beyond the gate`s a place
And it is hard to reach. You struggle there.

Looking out it is as if it`s drawn
On the old acid plate. Oak, the line
Of long smoke, these seem so near. They`re writ
On white their black. The only sound is crow.
But who has put Friday`s footprint down
On my untrodden shore of snow?

This is a landscape for the solitary and
Glances can be events. My mood is still,
Is warm but inward. I would not break it yet.